Hugh Henry Brackenridge, Dr. John Knight, John Slover

Narratives of a Late Expedition against the Indians

With an Account of the Barbarous Execution of Col. Crawford

Hugh Henry Brackenridge, Dr. John Knight, John Slover

Narratives of a Late Expedition against the Indians
With an Account of the Barbarous Execution of Col. Crawford

ISBN/EAN: 9783337292928

Printed in Europe, USA, Canada, Australia, Japan

Cover: Foto ©ninafisch / pixelio.de

More available books at **www.hansebooks.com**

NARRATIVES

OF A LATE

EXPEDITION

AGAINST THE

INDIANS;

WITH

An ACCOUNT of the BARBAROUS
EXECUTION of Col. CRAWFORD;

AND

The WONDERFUL ESCAPE of Dr. *Knight* and
John Slover from CAPTIVITY, in 1782.

PHILADELPHIA:
Printed by FRANCIS BAILEY, in Market Street.

M,DCC,LXXIII.

To the PUBLIC.

The two following narratives were tranfmitted for publication in September laft, but fhortly afterwards the
letter from fir Guy Carleton to his excellency general
Wafhington, informing that the favages had received orders to defift from their incurfions, gave reafon
to hope that there would be an end to their barbari-
ties. For this reafon it was not thought neceffary to
hold up to view what they had heretofore done. But
as they ftill continue their murders on our frontiers,
thefe narratives may be fervicable to induce our go-
vernments to take fome effectual fteps to chaftife and
reprefs them; as from hence they will fee that the nature of an Indian is fierce and cruel, and that an extirpation of them would be ufeful to the world, and
honourable to thofe who can effect it.

Mr. BAILEY,

Enclofed are two narratives; one of Dr. Knight, who
acted as furgeon in the expedition under col. Crawford; the other of John Slover: That of Dr. Knight
was written by himfelf at my requeft; that of Slover
was taken down by myfelf from his mouth as he re-
lated it. The man from his early and long captivity, amongft the Indians, though perfectly fenfible and
intelligent, yet cannot write. The character of Dr.
Knight is well known to to be that of a good man, of
great veracity, of a calm and deliberate mind, and
ufing no exaggeration in his account of any matter.
As a teftimony in favour of the veracity of Slover,
I thought proper to procure a certificate from the
clergyman to whofe church he belongs, and which is
as follows:

" I DO hereby certify that John Slover has been for
many years a regular member of the church under
my care, and is worthy of the higheft credit,
WILLIAM RENO."

Thefe narratives you will pleafe to publifh in your ufeful paper or in any other way you may judge proper.
I conceive the publication of them may anfwer a good
end in fhowing America, what have been the fuffer-
ings of fome of her citizens by the hands of the Indian allies of Britain. To thefe narratives I have
fubjoined fome obfervations which you may publifh
or omit as it may be convenient.
H. BRACKENRIDGE,

Pittfburgh, Aug. 3, 1782.

Dr. KNIGHT's Narrative.

'A BOUT the latter end of the month of March or the beginning of April, of the prefent year, the weftern Indians began to make incurfions upon the frontiers of Ohio, Wafhington, Youghagany, and Weftmoreland counties, which has been their conftant practice ever fince the commencement of the prefent war between the United States and Great Britain.

In confequence of thefe predatory invafions the principal officers of the abovementioned counties, namely, colonels Williamfon and Marfhall, tried every method in their power to fet on foot an expedition againft the Wyandot towns, which they could effect no other way than by giving all poffible encouragement to volunteers. The plan propofed was as follows: Every man furnifhing himfelf with a horfe, a gun, and one months provifion, fhould be exempted from two tours of militia duty. Likewife, that every one who had been plundured by the Indians, fhould, if the plunder could be found at their towns, have it again, proving it to be his property: and all horfes loft on the expedition by unavoidable accident were to be replaced by horfes taken in the enemy's country.

The time appointed for the rendezvous, or general meeting of the volunteers, was fixed to be on the 20th of May, and the place, the old Mingoe town on the weft fide of the river Ohio, about forty miles below Fort Pitt by land, and I think about 75 by water.

Col. Crawford was folicited by the general voice of thefe weftern counties and diftricts to command the expedition. He accordingly fet out as a volunteer and came to Fort Pitt two days before the time appointed for the affembling of the men. As there was no furgeon yet appointed to go with the expedition, colonel Crawford begged the favour of gen. Irvine to permit me to accompany him, (my confent having been previoufly

oufly afked) to which the general agreed provided col. Gibfon did not object.

Having obtained permiffion of the colonel I left Fort Pitt on Tuefday, May 1ft, and the next day about one in the afternoon arrived at the Mingoe bottom. The volunteers had not all croffed the river until Friday morning the 24th, they then diftributed themfelves into eighteen companies, choofing their captains by vote. There were chofen, alfo, one col commandant, four field and one brigade major. There were four hundred and fixty five who voted.

We began our march on Saturday May 25th, making almoft a due weft courfe, and on the fourth day reached the old Moravian town, upon the river Mufkingum about 60 miles from the river Ohio. Some of the men having loft their horfes on the night preceding, return ed home.

Tuefday the 28th in the evening, major Brenton and captain Bean went fome diftance from camp to reconnoitre: having gone about one quarter of a mile they faw two indians, upon whom they fired, and then returned to camp. This was the firft place in which we were difcovered, as we underftood afterwards.

On Thurfday the fourth of June, which was the eleventh day of our march, about one o'clock we came to the fpot where the town of Sandufky formerly ftood: the inhabitants had moved 18 miles lower down the creek, nearer the lower Sandufky; but as neither our guides or any who were with us, had known any thing of their removal, we began to conjecture there were no Indian towns nearer than the lower Sandufky, which was at leaft 40 miles diftant.

However, after refrefhing our horfes we advanced on in fearch of fome of their fettlements, but had fcarcely got the diftance of three or four miles from the old town when a number of our men expreffed their defire to return, fome of them alledging that they had only five days provifion; upon which the field officers and captains, determined, in council, to proceed that afternoon and no longer. Previous to the calling of this council, a fmall party of light horfe had been fent forward to reconnoitre.

I fhall here remark, by the way, that there are a great

great many extensive plains in that country: The woods in general grow very thin, and free from brush and underwood; so that light horsemen may advance a considerable distance before an army without being much exposed to the enemy.

Just as the council ended, an express returned from the above mentioned party of light horse with intelligence, "that they had been about three miles in front, and had seen a large body of Indians running towards them."—In a short time we saw the rest of the light horse, who joined us, and having gone one mile further met a number of Indians who had partly got possession of a piece of woods before us, whilst we were in the plains, but our men alighting from their horses and rushing into the woods soon obliged them to abandon that place.

The enemy being by this time reinforced flanked to the right, and part of them coming in our rear quickly made the action more serious. The firing continued very warm on both sides from four o'clock until the dusk of the evening, each party maintaining their ground. Next morning about six o'clock some guns were discharged at the distance of two or three hundred yards, which continued till day, doing little or no execution on either side.

The field officers then assembled and agreed, as the enemy were every moment increasing and we had already a number wounded, to retreat that night. The whole body was to form into three lines, keeping the wounded in the center. We had four killed and twenty three wounded, of the latter, seven very dangerously, on which account as many biers were got ready to carry them: most of the rest were slightly wounded and none so bad but they could ride on horseback. After dark the officers went on the out posts and brought in all the men as expeditiously as they could. Just as the troops were about to form several guns were fired by the enemy, upon which some of our men spoke out and said, our intention was discovered by the Indians who were firing alarm guns. Upon which some in front hurried off and the rest immediately followed, leaving the seven men that were dangerously wounded, some of whom however got off on horseback, by means of some

good

good friends, who waited for, and aſſiſted them.

We had not got a quarter of a mile from the field of action when I heard col. Crawford calling for his ſon John Crawford, his ſon in law major Harriſon, major Roſe and William Crawford, his nephews, upon which I came up and told him I believed they were before us—He aſked, was that the doctor?—I told him it was—he then replied, they were not in front, and begged of me not to leave him—I promiſed him I would not.

We then waited, and continued calling for theſe men till the troops had paſſed us. The colonel told me his horſe had almoſt given out, that he could not keep up with the troops, and wiſhed ſome of his beſt friends to remain with him: he then exclaimed againſt the militia for riding off in ſuch an irregular manner, and leaving ſome of the wounded behind, contrary to his orders. Preſently there came two men riding after us, one of them an old man, the other a lad: we enquired if they had ſeen any of the above perſons? they anſwered they had not.

By this time there was a very hot firing before us, and, as we judged, near where our main body muſt have been. Our courſe was then nearly ſouth-weſt, but changing it, we went north about two miles, the two men remaining in company with us. Judging ourſelves to be now out of the enemy's lines, we took a due eaſt courſe, taking care to keep at the diſtance of fifteen or twenty yards apart, and directing ourſelves by the north ſtar.

The old man often lagged behind and when this was the caſe never failed to call for us to halt for him. When we were near the Sanduſky Creek he fell one hundred yards behind, and bawled out, as uſual, for us to halt. While we were preparing to reprimand him for making a noiſe, I heard an Indian halloo, as I thought one hundred and fifty yards from the man and partly behind him; after this we did not hear the man call again neither did he ever come up to us any more. It was now paſt midnight, and about day break col. Crawford's and the young man's horſes gave out, and they left them. We purſued our journey eaſtward, and about two o'clock fell in with
capt.

capt. Biggs who had carried lieut. Aſhley from the field of action, who had been dangerouſly wounded. We then went on about the ſpace of an hour, when a heavy rain coming on we concluded it was beſt to encamp, as we were encumbered with the wounded officer. We then barked four or five trees, made an encampment and a fire and remained there all that night. Next morning we again proſecuted our journey, and having gone about three miles found a deer which had been recently killed. The meat was ſliced from the bones and bundled up in the ſkin with a tomahawk lying by it. We carried all with us and in advancing about one mile further eſpyed the ſmoke of a fire. We then gave the wounded officer into the charge of the young man, deſiring him to ſtay behind whilſt the colonel, the captain, and myſelf, walked up as cautiouſly as we could toward the fire. When we came to it, we concluded from ſeveral circumſtances ſome of our people had encamped there the preceding night. We then went about roaſting the veniſon, and when juſt about to march obſerved one of our men coming upon our tracks. He ſeemed at firſt very ſhy, but having called to him he came up and told us he was the perſon who had killed the deer, but upon hearing us come up, was afraid of Indians, hid it in a thicket and made off. Upon this we gave him ſome bread and roaſted veniſon, proceeded altogether on our journey and about two o'clock came upon the paths by which we had gone out. Capt. Biggs and myſelf did not think it ſafe to keep the road, but the colonel ſaid the Indians would not follow the troops farther than the plains, which we were then conſiderably paſt. As the wounded officer rode capt. Biggs' horſe I lent the captain mine; the colonel and myſelf went about one hundred yards in front, the captain and the wounded officer in the center, and the two young men behind. After we had travelled about one mile and a half, ſeveral Indians ſtarted up within fifteen or twenty ſteps of the colonel and me. As we at firſt diſcovered only three I immediately got behind a large black-oak, made ready my piece and raiſed it up to take fight, when the colonel called to me twice not to fire; upon that one of

the

[9]

the Indians ran up to the colonel and took him by the hand. The colonel then told me to put down my gun, which I did. At that inftant one of them came up to me whom I had formerly feen very often, called me doctor and took me by the hand. They were Delaware Indians of the Wingenim tribe. Captain Biggs fired amongft them but did no execution. They then told us, to call thefe people and make them come there, elfe they would go and kill them, which the colonel did, but they four got off and efcaped for that time. The colonel and I were then taken to the Indian camp, which was about half a mile from the place where we were captivated. On Sunday evening five Delawares who had pofted themfelves at fome diftance further on the road brought back to the camp, where we lay, captain Biggs' and lieutenant Afhley's fcalps, with an Indian fcalp which captain Bigg's had taken in the field of action: they alfo brought in Biggs' horfe and mine, they told us the two other men got away from them.

Monday morning the tenth of June we were paraded to march to Sandufky, about 33 miles diftant : they had eleven prifoners of us and four fcalps, the Indians being feventeen in number.

Col. Crawford was very defirous to fee a certain Simon Girty, who lived with the Indians, and was on this account permitted to go to town the fame night, with two warriors to guard him, having orders at the fame time to pafs by the place where the col. had turned out his horfe, that they might if poffible, find him. The reft of us were taken as far as the old town which was within eight miles of the new.

Tuefday morning the 11th, col. Crawford was brought out to us on purpofe to be marched in with the other prifoners. I afked the colonel if he had feen Mr. Girty?—He told me he had, and that Girty had promifed to do every thing in his power for him, but that the Indians were very much enraged againft the prifoners; particularly captain Pipe one of the chiefs: he likewife told me that Girty had informed him that his fon in law col. Harrifon and his nephew William Crawford, were made prifoners by the Shawanefe, but had been pardoned. This capt. Pipe had come from the towns

B   about

about an hour before col. Crawford, and had painted all the prifoners faces black.

As he was painting me he told me I fhould go to the Shawanefe towns and fee my friends. When the colonel arrived he painted him black alfo, told him he was glad to fee him, and that he would have him fhaved when he came to fee his friends at the Wyandot town. When we marched the col. and I were kept back between Pipe and Wyngenim, the two Delaware chiefs, the other nine prifoners were fent forward with another party of Indians. As we went along we faw four of the prifoners lying by the path tomahaked and fcalped fome of them were at the diftance of half a mile from each other. When we arrived within half a mile of the place where the colonel was executed, we overtook the five prifoners that remained alive: the Indians had caufed them to fit down on the ground, as they did alfo the colonel and me at fome diftance from them I was there given in charge to an Indian fellow to be taken to the Shawanefe towns.

In the place where we were now made to fit down there was a number of fquaws and boys who fell on the five prifoners and tomahawk'd them. There was a certain John M'Kinly amongft the prifonners, formerly an officer in the 13th Virginia regiment, whofe head on old fquaw cut off, and the Indians kicked it about upon the ground. The young indian fellows came often where the colonel and I were, and dafhed the fcalps in our faces. We were then conducted along toward the place where the colonel was afterwards executed: when we came within about half a mile of it Simon Girty met us, with feveral Indians on horfeback: he fpoke to the colonel, but as I was about one hundred and fifty yards behind could not hear what paffed between them.

Almoft every Indian we met ftruck us either with fticks or their fifts. Girty waited till I was brought up and afked, was that the doctor?—I told him, yes, and went toward him reaching out my hand, but he bid me begone and called me a damn'd rafcal, upon which the fellow who had me in charge pulled me along. Girty rode up after me and told me I was to go to the Shawanefe towns.

When

When we were come to the fire the colonel was ftripped naked, ordered to fit down by the fire and then
they beat him with fticks and their fifts. Prefently
after I was treated in the fame n.anner. They then
tied a rope to the foot of a poft about fifteen feet high,
bound the colonel's hands behind his back and faften-
ed the rope to the ligature between his wrifts. The
rope was long enough either for him to fit down or walk
round the poft once or twice and return the fame way.
The colonel then called to Girty and afked if they intended to burn him?—Girty anfwered, yes. The colonel faid he would take it all patiently. Upon this
capt. Pipe, a Delaware chief, made a fpeech to the Indians, viz. about thirty or forty men, fixty or feventy
fquaws and boys.

When the fpeech was finifhed they all yelled a hide-
ous and hearty affent to what had been faid. The Indian men then took up their guns and fhot powder into
the colonel's body, from his feet as far up as his neck.
I think not lefs than feventy loads were difcharged
upon his naked body. They then crowded about him,
and to the beft of my obfervation, cut off his ears:
when the throng had difperfed a little I faw the blood
running from both fides of his head in confequence
thereof.

The fire was about fix or feven yards from the
poft to which the colonel was tied: it was made of
fmall hickory poles, burnt quite through in the middle,
each end of the poles remaining about fix feet in length.
Three or four Indians by turns would take up, indivi-
dually, one of thefe burning pieces of wood and apply
it to his naked body, already burnt black with the powder. Thefe tormentors prefented themfelves on every
fide of him, fo that which ever way he ran round the
poft they met him with the burning faggots and poles.
Some of the fquaws took broad boards upon which they
would put a quantity of burning coals and hot embers
and throw on him, fo that in a fhort time he had nothing but coals of fire and hot afhes to walk upon.

In the midft of thefe extreme tortures he called to Simon Girty and begged of him to fhoot him; but Girty
making no anfwer he called to him again. Girty then,
by way of derifion, told the colonel he had no gun, at
the

the fame time turning about to an Indian who was behind him, laughed heartily, and by all his geſtures
ſeemed delighted at the horrid ſcene.

Girty then came up to me and bade me prepare for
death. He ſaid, however, I was not to die at that
place, but to be burnt at the Shawaneſe towns. He
ſwore by G—d I need not expect to eſcape death, but
ſhould ſuffer it in all its extremities.

He then obſerved that ſome priſoners had given him
to underſtand that if our people had him they would
not hurt him; for his part, he ſaid, he did not believe
it, but deſired to know my opinion of the matter; but
being at that time in great anguiſh and diſtreſs for the
torments the colonel was ſuffering before my eyes, as
well as the expectation of undergoing the ſame fate in
two days, I made little or no anſwer. He expreſſed a
great deal of ill will for col. Gibſon, and ſaid he was one
of his greateſt enemies, and more to the ſame purpoſe,
to all which I paid very little attention.

Col. Crawford at this period of his ſufferings beſought
the Almighty to have mercy on his ſoul, ſpoke very
low, and bore his torments with the moſt manly forti-
tude. He continued in all the extremities of pain for
an hour and three quarters or two hours longer, as
near as I can judge, when at laſt being almoſt ſpent,
he lay down on his belly: they then ſcalped him and
repeatedly threw the ſcalp in my face, telling me "that
was my great captain."—An old ſquaw (whoſe appearance every way anſwered the ideas people entertain of
the Devil) got a board, took a parcel of coals and aſhes
and laid them on his back and head after he had been
ſcalped: he then raiſed himſelf upon his feet and began
to walk round the poſt: they next put a burning ſtick
to him as uſual, but he ſeemed more inſenſible of pain
than before.

The Indian fellow who had me in charge now took
me away to capt. Pipes' houſe, about three quarters of
a mile from the place of the colonel's execution. I
was bound all night and thus, prevented from ſeeing the
laſt of the horrid ſpectacle. Next morning, being June
12th, the Indian untied me, painted me black, and we
ſet off for the Shawaneſe town, which he told me was
ſomewhat leſs than forty miles from that place. We
ſoon

soon came to the spot where the colonel had been burnt, as it was partly in our way; I saw his bones laying amongst the remains of the fire, almost burnt to ashes, I suppose after he was dead they had laid his body on the fire.

The Indian told me, that was my Big Captain and gave the scalp halloo. He was on horseback and drove me before him.

I pretended to this Indian I was ignorant of the death I was to die at the Shawanese town, affected as chearful a countinance as possible and asked him if we were not to live together as brothers in one house when we should get to the town?—He seemed well pleased, and said, yes. He then asked me if I could make a wigwam?—I told him, I could—he then seemed more friendly —we went that day as near as I can judge about 25 miles, the course partly southwest—The Indian told me we should next day come to the town the sun being in such a direction, pointing nearly south. At night when we went to rest I attempted very often to unty myself but the Indian was extremely vigilant and scarce ever shut his eyes that night. About day break he got up and untied me: he next began to mend up the fire and as the gnats were troublesome I asked him if I should make a smoke behind him?—he said, yes. I then took the end of a dogwood fork which had been burnt down to about 18 inches long: it was the longest stick I could find, yet too small for the purpose I had in view: then I picked up another smaller stick and taking a coal of fire between them went behind him: then turning suddenly about, I struck him on the head with all the force I was master of; which so stunned him that he fell forwards with both his hands into the fire, but seeing him recover and get up, I siezed his gun while he ran off howling in a most fearful manner—I followed him with a determination to shoot him down, but pulling back the cock of the gun with too great violence I believe I broke the main spring. I pursued him, however, about thirty yards still endeavouring to fire the gun, but could not; then going back to the fire I took his blanket, a pair of new mokkisons, his hoppes, powder horn, bullet bag, (together with the gun) and marched off, directing my course toward the five o'clock mark; about half an

hour

hour before sunset I came to the plains which I think are about sixteen miles wide. I laid me down in a thicket till dark and then by the assistance of the north star made my way through them and got into the woods before morning. I proceeded on the next day and about noon crossed the paths by which our troops had gone out: these paths are nearly east and west but I went due north all that afternoon with a view to avoid the enemy.

In the evening I began to be very faint, and no wonder; I had been six days prisoner; the last two days of which I had eat nothing and but very little the first three or four: there were wild goosberries in abundance in the woods, but being unripe required mastication, which at that time I was not able to perform on account of a blow received from an Indian on the jaw with the back of a tomahawk: there was a weed that grew plentifully in that place, the juice of which I knew to be grateful and nourishing; I gathered a bundle of the same, took up my lodging under a large spreading beech tree and having sucked plentifully of the juice, went to sleep. Next day I made a due east course which I generally kept the rest of my journey. I often imagined my gun was only wood bound and tried every method I could devise to unscrew the lock but never could effect it having no knife nor any thing fitting for the purpose; I had now the satisfaction to find my jaw began to mend and in four or five days could chew any vegetable proper for nourishment, but finding my gun only a useless burden left her in the wilderness. I had no apparatus for making fire to sleep by so that I could get but little rest for the gnats and musketoes; there are likewise a great many swamps in the beach ridge which occasioned me very often to lie wet: this ridge through which I travelled is about 20 miles broad, the ground in general very level and rich, free from shrubs and brush: there are, however, very few springs, yet wells might easily be dug in all parts of that ridge; the timber on it is very lofty, but it is no easy matter to make a straight course through the same, the moss growing as high upon the south side of the trees as on the north. There are a great many white oaks, ash and hickory trees that grow among the beach timber; there

are

are likewife fome places on the ridge, perhaps for three
or four continued miles where there is little or no beech,
and in fuch fpots, black, white oak, afh and hickory a-
bound. Sugar trees grow there alfo to a very great bulk:
the foil is remarkably good, the ground a little afcend-
ing and defending with fome fmall rivulets and a few
fprings. When I got out of the beech ridge and nearer
the river Mufkingum the lands were more broken but
equally rich with thofe before mentioned, and abound-
ing with brooks and fprings of water: there are alfo
feveral fmall creeks that empty into that river, the bed
of which is more than a mile wide in many places: the
woods confift of white and black oaks, walnut, hickory
and fugar tree in the greateft abundance. In all parts
of the country through which I came the game was
very plenty, that is to fay, deer, turkies and pheafants,
I likewife faw a great many veftiges of bears and fome
elks.

I croffed the river Mufkingum about three or four
miles below Fort Laurence, and croffing all paths aim-
ed for the Ohio river. All this time my food was goofe-
berries, young nettles, the juice of herbs, a few fervice berries, and fome May apples, likewife, two young
blackbirds and a turripine, which I devoured raw.
When my food fat heavy on my ftomach, I ufed to eat
a little wild ginger which put all to rights.

I came upon Ohio river about five miles below fort
M'Intofh, in the evening of the 21ft day after I had
made my efcape, and on the twenty fecond, about feven
o'clock in the morning, being the fourth day of July,
arrived fafe, though very much fatigued, at the fort.

A Short MEMOIR of the within mentioned Col. CRAWFORD.

COL. CRAWFORD, was about 50 years of age, had been an old warrior against the savages. He distinguished himself early as a volunteer in the last war, and was taken notice of by colonel (now general) Washington, who procured for him the commission of ensign. As a partisan he showed himself very active, and was greatly successful: He took several Indian towns, and did great service in scouting, patrolling and defending the frontiers. At the commencement of this war he raised a regiment in the back country by his own exertions: He had the commission of colonel in the continental army, and acted bravely on several occasions in the years 1776, 1777, and at other times. He held his commission at the time he took command of the militia, in the aforesaid expedition against the Indians: most probably he had it with him when he was taken: He was a man of good judgment, singular good nature, and great humanity, and remarkable for his hospitality; few strangers coming to the western country, and not spending some days at the crossings of the Yochaghany river where he lived; no man therefore could be more regretted.

The Narrative of John Slover.

HAVING in the laſt war been a priſoner amongſt the Indians many years, and ſo being well acquainted with the country weſt of the Ohio I was employed as a guide in the expedition under col. William Crawford againſt the Indian towns on or near the river Sanduſky. It will be unneceſſary for me to relate what is ſo well known, the circumſtances and unfortunate event of that expedition; it will be ſufficient to obſerve, that having on Tueſday the fourth of June fought the enemy near Sanduſky, we lay that night in our camp, and the next day fired on each other at the diſtance of three hundred yards, doing little or no execution. In the evening of that day it was propoſed by col. Crawford, as I have been ſince informed, to draw off with order; but at the moment of our retreat the Indians (who had probably perceived that we were about to retire) firing alarm guns, our men broke and rode off in confuſion, treading down thoſe who were on foot, and leaving the wounded men who ſupplicated to be taken with them.

I was with ſome others on the rear of our troops feeding our horſes in the glade, when our men began to break: The main body of our people had paſſed by me a conſiderable diſtance before I was ready to ſet out. I overtook them before they croſſed the glade, and was advanced almoſt in front. The company in which I was had ſeparated from me, and had endeavoured to paſs a morafs; for coming up I found their horſes had ſtuck faſt in the morafs, and endeavouring to paſs, mine alſo in a ſhort time ſtuck faſt I ought to have ſaid, the company of five or ſix men with which I had been immediately connected; and who were ſome diſtance to the right of the main body, had ſeparated from me, &c. I try'd a long time to diſengage my horſe, until I could hear the enemy juſt behind me and on each ſide, but in vain. Here then I was obliged to leave him. The morafs was ſo unſtable that I was to the middle in it,

C

and

and it was with the greateſt difficulty that I got acroſs it but which having at length done, I came up with the ſix men who had left their horſes in the ſame manner I had done; two of theſe, my companions, having loſt their guns.

We travelled that night making our courſe towards Detroit, with a view to ſhun the enemy, who we conceived to have taken the paths by which the main body of our people had retreated. Juſt before day we got into a ſecond deep moraſs, and were under the neceſſity of detaining until it was light to ſee our way through it. The whole of this day we travelled toward the Shawaneſe towns, with a view of throwing ourſelves ſtill far her out of the ſearch of the enemy. About ten o'clock this day we ſat down to eat a little, having taſted nothing from Tueſday, the day of our engagement, until this time which was on Thurſday; and now the only thing we had to eat was a ſcrap of pork to each. We had ſat down juſt by a warrior's path which we had not ſuſpected, when eight or nine warriors appeared Running off haſtily we left our baggage and proviſions, but were not diſcovered by the party; for ſkulking ſome time in the graſs and buſhes, we returned to the place and recovered our baggage. The warriors had hallooed as they paſſed, and were anſwered by others on our flanks

In our journey through the glades, or wide extended dry meadows, about twelve o'clock this day we diſcovered a party of Indians in front, but ſkulking in the graſs and buſhes were not perceived by them. In theſe glades we were in great danger, as we could be ſeen at a great diſtance. In the afternoon of this day there fell a heavy rain, the coldeſt I ever felt. We halted while it rained, and then travelling on we ſaw a party of the enemy about two hundred yards before us, but hiding ourſelves in the buſhes, we had again the good fortune not to be diſcovered. This night we got out of the glades, having in the night croſſed the paths by which we had advanced to Sanduſky. It was our deſign to leave all theſe paths to the right, and to come in by the Tuſcarawas. We ſhould have made a much greater progreſs, had it not been for two of our companions who

who were lame; the one having his foot burnt, the other with a fwelling in his knee of a rheumatic nature.

On this day, which was the fecond after the retreat, one of our company, the perfon affected with the rheumatic fwelling, was left behind fome diftance in a fwamp. Waiting for him fome time we faw him coming within one hundred yards, as I fat on the body of an old tree mending my mokkifins, but taking my eye from him I faw him no more. He had not obferved our tracks, but had gone a different way. We whiftled on our chargers, and afterwards hallooed for him, but in vain. Neverthelefs he was fortunate in miffing us, for he afterwards came fafe into Wheeling *. We travelled on until night, and were on the waters of Mufkingum from the middle of this day.

Having catched a fawn this day we made a fire in the evening, and had a repaft, having in the mean time eat nothing but the fmall bit of pork I mentioned before. We fet off at break of day. About nine o'clock the third day we fell in with a party of the enemy about twenty miles from the Tufcarawas, which is about 135 miles from fort Pitt. They had come upon our tracks, or had been on our flanks, and difcovered us, and then having got before had way laid us, and fired before we perceived them. At the firft fire one of my companions fell before me, and another juft behind; thefe two had guns: there were fix men in company, and four guns, two of thefe rendered ufelefs by reafon of the wet, when coming through the fwamp the firft night; we had tryed to difcharge them, but could not. When the indians fired I ran to a tree; but an Indian prefenting himfelf fifteen yards before me, defired me to deliver myfelf up and I fhould not be hurt: My gun was in good order, but apprehending the enemy behind might difcharge their pieces at me, I did not rifk firing, which I had afterwards reafon to regret, when I found what was to be my fate, and that the Indian who was before me and prefented his gun, was one of thofe who had juft before fired. Two of my companions were taken with

* This is a poft of ours on the Ohio, about 70 miles below Fort Pitt.

with me in the fame manner, the Indians affuring us we fhould not be hurt. But one in company, James Paul, who had a gun in order made his efcape, and has fince come into Wheeling. One of thefe Indians knew me, and was of the party by whom I was taken in the laft war. He came up and fpoke to me calling me by my Indian name, Mannuchcothee, and upbraiding me for coming to war againft them. I will take a moment here to relate fome particulars of my firft captivity, and my life fince.

I was taken from New River in Virginia by the Miamefe, a nation of Indians by us called the Pifts, amongft whom I lived fix years; afterwards being fold to a Delaware, and by him put into the hands of a trader, I was carried amongft the Shawanefe, with whom I continued fix years; fo that my whole time amongft thefe nations was twelve years, that is, from the eighth to the twentieth year of my age. At the treaty at Fort Pitt in the fall preceding what is called Dunmore's war, which, if I am right was in the year 1773, I came in with the Shawanefe nation to the treaty, and meeting with fome of my relations at that place was by them follicited to relinquifh the life of a favage, which I did with fome reluctance, this manner of life having become natural to me, inafmuch as I had fcarcely known any other. I enlifted as a foldier in the continental army at the commencement of the prefent war, and ferved fifteen months. Having been properly difcharged I have fince married, have a family, and am in communion with the church

To return: The party by whom we were made prifoners had taken fome horfes, and left them at the glades we had paffed the day before They had followed on our trafts from thefe glades; on our return to which we found the horfes and rode We were carried to Wachatcmakak, a town of the Mingoes and Shawanefe. I think it was on the third day we reached the town, which when we were approaching, the Indians, in whofe cuftody we were, began to look four, having been kind to us before, and given us a little meat and flour to eat, which they had found or taken from fome of our men on their retreat. This
[town

town is fmall, and we were told was about two miles
diftant from the main town to which they meant to
carry us.

The inhabitants from this town came out with clubs
and tomhawks, ftruck beat and abufed us greatly.
One of my two companions they feized, and having
ftripped him naked blacked him with coal and water:
This was the fign of being burnt the man feemed to
furmife it, and fhed tears. He afked me the meaning
of his being blacked; but I was forbid by the enemy
in their own language to tell him what was intended.
In Englifh which they fpoke eafily, having been often
at Fort Pitt, they affured him he was not to be hurt.
I know of no reafon for making him the firft objeft of
their cruelty, unlefs it was that he was the oldeft.

A warrior had been fent to the greater town to ac-
quaint them with our coming, and prepare them for
the frolic; for on our coming to it, the inhabitants
came out with guns, clubs and tomhawks. We were
told that we had to run to the council houfe, about
three hundred yards. The man that was blacked
was about twenty yards before us, in running the
gauntlet: They made him their pr ncipal objeft, men,
women and children beating him, and thofe who had
guns firing loads of powder on him as he ran naked,
putting the muzzles of the guns to his body, fhout-
ing, hallooing and beating their drums in the mean
time.

The unhappy man had reached the door of the council houfe, beat and wounded in a manner fhocking to
the fight; for having arrived before him we had it in
our power to view the fpeftacle: it was indeed the moft
horrid that can be conceived: they had cut him with
their tomhawks, fhot his body black, burnt it into holes
with loads of powder blown into him; a large wadding
had made a wound in his fhoulder whence the blood
gufhed.

Agreeable to the d claration of the enemy when he
firft fet out he had reafon to think himfelf fecure when
he had reached the door of the council houfe. This
feemed to be his hope, for coming up with great ftrug-
gling and endeavour, he laid hold of the door but was
pulled

pulled back and drawn away by them ; finding they intended no mercy, but putting him to death he attempted several times to fnatch or lay hold of fome of their tomhawks, but being weak could not effect it. We faw him borne off and they were a long time beating, wounding, purfuing and killing him.

That fame evening I faw the dead body of this man clofe by the council houfe. It was mangled cruelly and the blood mingled with the powder was rendered black. The fame evening I faw him, after he had been cut into pieces and his limbs and his head about two hundred yards on the outfide of the town put on poles. That evening alfo I faw the bodies of three others in the fame black and mangled condition : thefe I was told had been put to death the fame day and juft before we had reached the town. Their bodies as they lay were black, bloody, burnt with powder ; two of thefe were Harrifon * and young Crawford †. I knew the vifage of col. Harrifon, and I faw his cloathing and that of young Crawford, at the town. They brought horfes to me and afked if I knew them ?—I faid they were Harrifons and Crawfords. They faid they were.

The third of thefe men I did not know, but believe to have been col. M,Cleland, the third in command on the expedition.

The

---

* This was col. Harrifon, fon in law to col. Crawford one of the firft men in the weftern country : he had been greatly active on many occafions in devifing meafure for the defence of the frontiers, and his character as a citizen in every way, tho' a young man, diftinguifhed and refpectable. He had been a magiftrate under the jurifdiction of Virginia, and I believe a delegate to the affembly of that ftate. I knew no man with whofe grave, fedate manners, prudent conduct, good fenfe and public fpirit on all occafions I was more pleafed H. B.

† This was a fon to col. Crawford. I do not remember to have feen him, nor was I acquainted with his character before the expedition, but have fince been informed univerfally that he was a young man greatly and defervedly efteemed as a foldier and as a citizen.
H. B.

The next day the bodies of thefe men were dragged to the outfide of the town, and their carcafes being given to the dogs, their limbs and heads were ftuck on poles.

My furviving companion fhortly after we had reached the council houfe was fent to another town, and I prefume he was burnt or executed in the fame manner.

In the evening the men affembled in the council houfe: this is a large building about fifty yards in length and about twenty five yards wide; and about fixteen feet in height, built of fplit poles covered with bark: their firft object was to examine me, which they could do in their own language, inafmuch as I could fpeak the Miame, Shawanefe and Delaware languages, which I had learned during my early captivity in the laft war: I found I had not forgotten thefe languages, efpecially the two former, as well as my native tongue.

They began with interrogating me concerning the fituation of our country, what were our provifions? our numbers? the ftate of the war between us and Britain? I informed them Cornwallis had been taken, which next day, when Matthew Elliot * with James Girty * came, he affirmed to be a lie, and the Indians feemed to give full credit to his declaration.

Hitherto I had been treated with fome appearance of kindnefs, but now the enemy began to alter their behaviour towards me. Girty had informed them, that when he afked me how I liked to live there, I had faid that I intended to take the firft opportunity to take a fcalp and run off. It was, to be fure, very probable that if I had fuch intention, I would communicate it to him. Another man came to me and told me a ftory of his having lived on the fouth branch of Potowmac in Virginia, and having three brothers there, he pretended he wanted to get away, but I fufpected his defign;

** Thefe men, Elliot and Girty, were inhabitants of the weftern country and fince the commencement of the war, having for fome time profeffed an attachment to America, went off to the Indians. They are of that horrid brood called Refugees, and whom the Devil has long fince marked for his own property.

sign; neverthelefs he reported that I had confented to go. In the mean time I was not tyed, and could have efcaped, but having nothing to put on my feet, I waited fome time longer to provide for this.

I was invited every night to the war dances, which they ufually continued until almoft day. I could not comply with their defire, believing thefe things to be the fervice of the devil.

The council lafted fifteen days; from fifty to one hundred warriors being ufually in council, and fometimes more. Every warrior is admitted to thefe councils; but only the chiefs or head warriors have the privilege of fpeaking. The head warriors are accounted fuch from the number of fcalps and prifoners they have taken.

The third day M'Kee * was in council, and afterwards was generally prefent. He fpoke little, and did not afk any quefions or fpeak to me at all. He lives about two miles out of the town, has a houfe built of fquared logs with a fhingled roof; he was dreffed in gold laced cloths. I had feen him at the former town through which I paffed.

I think it was on the laft day of the council, fave one, that a fpeech came from Detroit, brought by a warrior who had been counfelling with the commanding officer at that place. The fpeech had been long expeƈted, and was in anfwer to one fometime before fent from the town to Detroit: It was in a belt of Wampum, and began with addreffing them, " My children," and enquiring why they continued to take prifoners? "Provifions are fcarce; when prifoners are brought in we are obliged to maintain them, and ftill fome of them are running away, and carrying tidings of our affairs. When any of your people fall into the hands of the rebels they fhow no mercy: why then fhould you take prifoners? Take no more prifoners, my children, of any fort; man, woman or child."

Two

* This man before the war was an Indian agent for the Britifh. He was put on parole, broke it, went to the Indians and has fince continued violently to incite them to make war againft us.

Two days after a party of every nation that was near being collected, it was determined on to take no more prisoners of any fort. They had held a large council, and the determination was, that if it were possible they could find a child of a span or three inches long, they would show no mercy to it. At the conclusion of the council it was agreed upon by all the tribes present, viz: the Tawaws, Chiappawaws, the Wiondots, the Mingoes, the Delawares, the Shawanese, the Munfes, and a part of the Cherokees, that should any of the nations who were not present take any prisoner, these would rise against them, take away the prisoners and put them to death.

In the course of these deliberations I understood what was said perfectly. They laid plans against our settlements of Kentucky, the Falls, and towards Wheeling. These it will be unnecessary for me to mention in this narrative, more especially as the Indians finding me to have escaped, and knowing that I would not fail to communicate these designs, will be led to alter their resolutions.

There was one council held at which I was not present: The warriors had sent for me as usual, but the squaw with whom I lived would not suffer me to go, but hid me under a large quantity of skins. It may have been from an unwillingness that I should hear in council the determination with respect to me, that I should be burnt.

About this time twelve men were brought in from Kentucky, three of whom were burnt on this day; the remainder were distributed to other towns, and all, as the Indians informed me, were burnt. This was after the speech came from Detroit.

On this day also I saw an Indian who had just come into town, and who said that the prisoner he was bringing to be burnt, and who he said was a doctor, had made his escape from him. I knew this must have been Dr. Knight, who went as surgeon of the expedition. The Indian had a wound four inches long in his head, which he acknowledged the doctor had given him: he was cut to the scull. His story was, that he had untied the doctor, being asked by him to do so, the doctor promising that he would not go away; that while

D   he

he was employed in kindling the fire, the doctor snatch-
ed up the gun, had come behind and struck him; that
he then made a stroke at the doctor with his knife,
which he laid hold of, and his fingers were cut almost
off, the knife being drawn through his hand: that he
gave the doctor two stabs, one in the belly, the other
in the back; said the doctor was a great, big, tall,
strong man. Being now adopted in an Indian family,
and having some confidence for my safety, I took the
liberty to contradict this, and said that I knew the doctor, who was a weak, little man. The other warriors
laughed immoderately, and did not seem to credit him*.
At this time I was told that col. Crawford was burnt,
and they greatly exulted over it.

The day after the council I have mentioned, about
forty warriors accompanied by George Girty came
early in the morning round the house where I was. The
squaw gave me up; I was sitting before the door of the
house; they put a rope round my neck, tyed my arms
behind my back, stripped me naked, and blacked me
in the usual manner. George Girty as soon as I was
tyed, damned me, and said that I now should get what
I had deserved many years. I was led away to a town
distant about five miles, to which a messenger had been
dispatched to desire them to prepare to receive me:
Arriving at this town I was beaten with clubs and the
pipe ends of their tomhawks, and was kept for some
time tied to a tree before a house door. In the mean
while the inhabitants set out to another town about two
miles distant, where I was to be burnt, and where I arrived about three o'clock in the afternoon.

Here also was a council house, part of it covered and
part of it without a roof. In the part of it where no
cover was, but only sides built up, there stood a post
about sixteen feet in height, and in the middle of the
house around the post, there were three piles of wood
built about three feet high and four feet from the post.
Being

* It is well known that Mr. Slover mentioned these
circumstances at his first coming into Wheeling, and
before he could have known the relation of the doctor,
so that this is an evidence of the truth of the doctor's
account, and of his own.   H. B.

Being brought to the post my arms were tyed behind me, and the thong or cord with which they were bound was fastened to the post; a rope also was put about my neck, and tyed to the post about four feet above my head. During the time they were tying me, piles of wood were kindled and began to flame.

Death by burning, which appeared to be now my fate, I had resolved to sustain with patience. The divine grace of God had made it less alarming to me; for on my way this day I had been greatly exercised in regard to my latter end. I knew myself to have been a regular member of the church, and to have sought repentance for my sins; but though I had often heard of the faith of assurance, had known nothing of it; but early this day, instantaneously by a change wrought upon me, sudden and perceivable as lightning, an assurance of my peace made with God, sprung up in my mind. The following words were the subject of my meditation—" In peace thou shalt see God. Fear not those who can kill the body. In peace shalt thou depart." I was on this occasion by a confidence in mind. not to be resisted, fully assured of my salvation: This being the case, I was willing, satisfied, and glad to die.

I was tyed to the post, as I have already said, and the flame was now kindled. The day was clear, not a cloud to be seen; if there were clouds low in the horison, the sides of the house prevented me from seeing them, but I heard no thunder, or observed any sign of approaching rain. Just as the fire of one pile began to blaze, the wind rose; from the time they began to kindle the fire and to tie me to the post, until the wind began to blow, was about fifteen minutes. The wind blew a hurricane, and the rain followed in less than three minutes. The rain fell violent; and the fire, though it began to blaze considerably, was instantly extinguished. The rain lasted about a quarter of an hour.

When it was over the savages stood amazed, and were a long time silent. At last one said, We will let him alone till morning, and take a whole days frolic in burning him. The sun at this time was about three hours high. It was agreed upon, and the rope about my neck was untied, and making me sit down, they
began

began to dance around me. They continued dancing in this manner until eleven o'clock at night; in the mean time, beating, kicking, and wounding me with their tomhawks and clubs †.

At laſt one of the warriors, the Half Moon, aſked me if I was ſleepy? I anſwered, Yes. The head warrior then choſe out three men to take care of me. I was taken to a block houſe; my arms were tied until the cord was hid in the fleſh; they were tied in two places, round the wriſt and above the elbows. A rope was faſtened about my neck, and tied to a beam of the houſe, but permitting me to lie down on a board. The three warriors were conſtantly harraſſing and troubling me, ſaying, " How will you like to eat fire to morrow— you will kill no more Indians now." I was in expectation of their going to ſleep; when at length, about an hour before day break, two laid down; the third ſmoked a pipe, talked to me, and aſked the ſame painful queſtions. About half an hour after he alſo laid down, and I heard him begin to ſnore. Inſtantly I went to work, and as my arms were perfectly dead with the cord, I laid myſelf down upon my right arm which was behind my back, and keepiug it faſt with my fingers, which had ſtill ſome life and ſtrength, I ſlipped the cord from my left arm over my elbow and my wriſt. One of the warriors now got up and ſtirred the fire: I was apprehenſive that I ſhould be examined, and thought it was over with me; but my hopes revived when now he lay down again. I then attempted to unlooſe the rope about my neck, tryed to gnaw it but in vain, as it was as thick as my thumb and as hard as iron, being made of a buffaloe hide: I wrought with it a long time, gave it out, and could ſee no relief. At this time I ſaw day break and heard the cock crow: I made a ſecond attempt almoſt without hope, pulling the rope by putting my fingers between my neck and it, and to

my

† I obſerved marks on the man when I ſaw him, which was eight or ten days after he came in, particularly a wound above his right eye brow, which he had received with the pipe end of a tomhawk; but his back and body generally had been injured.   H. B.

my great furprife it came eafily untyed: it was a noofe with two or three knots tyed over it.

I ftept over the warriors as they lay, and having got out of the houfe looked back to fee if there was any difturbance; I then ran through the town into a corn field; in my way I faw a fquaw with four or five children lying afleep under a tree: going a different way into the field I untyed my arm which was greatly fwelled and turned black: having obferved a number of horfes in the glade as I ran through it, I went back to catch one, and on my way found a piece of an old rug or quilt hanging on a fence which I took with me: having caught the horfe, the rope with which I had been tyed ferving for a hal-ter, I rode off: the horfe was ftrong and fwift, and the woods being open and the country level, about ten o'clock that day I croffed the Siota river at a place by computation fifty full miles from the town. I had rode about twenty five miles on this fide Siota by three o'clock in the afternoon, when the horfe began to fail and could no longer go on a trot. I inftantly left him and on foot ran about twenty miles farther that day, mak-ing in the whole the diftance of near one hundred miles, In the evening I heard hallooing behind me and for this reafon did not halt until about ten o'clock at night, when I fat down, was extremely fick and vomited; but when the moon rofe which might have been about two hours after, I went on and travelled until day.

During the night I had a path, but in the morning judged it prudent to forfake the path and take a ridge for the diftance of fifteen miles, in a line at right angles to my courfe, putting back as I went along with a ftick the weeds which I had bended, left I fhould be track'd by the enemy. I lay the next night on the waters of Mufkingum: the nettles had been troublefome to me after my croffing the Siota, having nothing to defend myfelf but the piece of a rug which I had found, and which while I rode I ufed under me by way of faddle; the briars and thorns were now painful to and prevent-ed me from travelling in the night until the moon ap-peared: In the mean time I was hindred from fleeping by the mufketoes, for even in the day I was under the neceffity of travelling with a handful of bufhes to brufh them from my body.

The

The fecond night I reached Cufhakim; next day came to Newcomer's town, where I got about feven rafberries, which were the firft thing I ate from the morning in which the Indians had taken me to burn me until this time, which was now about three o'clock: the fourth day I felt hunger very little, but was extremely weak; I fwam Mufkingum river at Oldcomers town, the river being about two hundred yards wide, having reached the bank I fat down, looked back and thought I had a ftart of the indians if any fhould purfue. That evening I travelled about five miles, next day came to Stillwater a fmall river, in a branch of which I got two fmall crafifh to eat: Next night I lay within five miles of Wheeling, but had not flept a wink during this whole time, being rendered impoffible by the mufketoes, which it was my conftant employment to brufh away. Next day came to Wheeling and faw a man on the ifland in the Ohio oppofite to that poft, and calling to him and afking for particular perfons who had been on the expedition, and telling him I was Slover, at length, with great difficulty, he was perfuaded to come over and bring me acrofs in his canoe *.

* It has been faid, that the putting to death the Moravian Indians has been the caufe of the cruelties practifed on the prifoners taken at Sandufky. But though this has been made an excufe by the refugees amongft the favages, and by the Britifh, yet it muft be well known, that it has been the cuftom of the favages at all times. I have it from colonel John Campbell, who is lately from Chamblee, where he has been in confinement a long time, and was taken on the Ohio fome years ago, that two men who were taken with him were put to death at the Shawnefe towns in the fame manner in which [Harrifon was afterwards executed, viz. by blowing powder into their bodies. A large load blowed into the body of one of thefe men, reached his kidneys; the pain throwing him into rage and madnefs, the favages were uncommonly diverted with the violence of his exclamation and geftures; boys of the town particularly following him, and confidering it as excellent fport. In the evening his head was cut off, and an end put to his mifery. Col. Campbell himfelf was
led

led out to make fport of the fame kind, but was faved, by the interpofition, I think, of Elliot.

At the fame time, though I would ftrike away this excufe which is urged for the favages, I am far from approving the Moravian flaughter. Doubtlefs the exiftence of that body of people in our neighbourhood, was of difadvantage, as they were under the neceffity of receiving and refrefhing the Sandufky favages as they came to war, and as they returned; and as no doubt fome amongft them communicated intelligence of any expedition on foot againft the enemy. I am alfo difpofed to believe, that the greater part of the men put to death were warriors; this appears from the teftimony of one againft another, from the confeffion of many, from their finging the war fong when ordered out to be tomhawked, from the cut and painting of their hair, and from other circumftances. The greater part of the Moravian men who were really peaceable or well affected to us, having been carried off the fall before, and ftill detained at Sandufky. But the putting to death the women and children, who fang hymns at their execution, muft be confidered as unjuftifiable inexcufable homicide; and that the colonel who commanded the party, and who is faid perfeveringly, contrary to the remonftrances of officers prefent, to have enjoined the perpetration of the act, has not yet been called to an account, is a difgrace to the ftate of Pennfylvania.

H. BRACKENRIDGE.

Mr. B A I L E Y,

WITH the narrative enclofed, I fubjoin fome obfervations with regard to the animals, vulgarly called Indians. It is not my intention to write any laboured effay ; for at fo great a diftance from the city, and fo long unaccuftomed to write, I have fcarcely refolution to put pen to paper. Having an opportunity to know fomething of the character of this race of men, from the deeds they perpetrate daily around me, I think proper to fay fomething on the fubject ; indeed feveral years ago, and before I left your city, I had thought different from fome others with refpect to the right of foil, and the propriety of forming treaties and making peace with them. In the United States Magazine, in the year 1779, I publifhed a differtation denying them to have a right to the foil: I perceive a writer in your very elegant and ufeful paper, has taken up the fame fubject, under the fignature of Caractacus, and unanfwerably fhown, that their claim to the extenfive countries of America, is wild and inadmiffible: I will take the liberty in this place, to purfue this fubject a little.

On what is their claim founded ?—Occupancy. A wild Indian with his fkin painted red, and a feather through his nofe, has fet his foot on the broad continent of North and South America: a fecond wild Indian with his ears cut in ringlets, or his nofe flit like a fwine or a malefactor, alfo fets his foot on the fame extenfive tract of foil: Let the firft Indian make a talk to his brother, and bid him take his foot off the continent, for he being firft upon it, had occupied the whole, to kill buffaloes, and tall elks with long horns. This claim, in the reafoning of fome men would be juft, and the fecond favage ought to depart in his canoe, and feek a continent where no prior occupant claimed the foil. Is this claim of occupancy of a very early date? When Noah's three fons, Shem, Ham, and Japhet, went out to the three quarters of the old world, Ham to Africa, Shem to Afia, and Japhet to Europe, did each claim a quarter of the world for his refidence? Suppofe Ham to have fpent his time fifhing or gathering oyfiers in the Red Sea, never once ftretching his leg in a long walk to fee his vaft dominions, from the mouth of the Nile, acrofs the mountains of Ethiopia and the river Niger

to

to the cape of Good Hope, where the Hottentotts, a cleanly people, now ftray; or fuppofing him, like a Scots pedlar, to have travelled over many thoufand leagues of that country: would this give him a right to the foil?—In the opinion of fome men it would eftablifh an exclufive right. Let a man in more modern times take a journey or voyage like Patrick Kennedy and others, to the heads of the Miffifippi or Miffouri rivers, would he gain a right ever after to exclude all perfons from drinking the water of thefe ftreams? Might not a fecond Adam make a talk to them and fay, is the whole of this water neceffary to allay your thirft, and may not I alfo drink of it?

The whole of this earth was given to man, and all defcendents of Adam have a right to fhare it equally. There is no right of primogeniture in the laws of nature and of nations. There is reafon that a tall man, fuch as the chaplain in the American army we call the High Prieft, fhould have a larger fpot of ground to ftretch himfelf upon; or that a man with a big belly, like a goodly alderman of London, fhould have a larger garden to produce beans and cabbage for his appetite, but that an agile, nimble runner, like an Indian called the Big Cat, at Fort Pitt, fhould have more than his neighbours becaufe he has traverfed a greater fpace, I can fee no reafon.

I have converfed with fome perfons and found their miftakes on this fubject, to arife from a view of claims by individuals in a ftate of fociety, fome holding a greater proportion of the foil than others; but this is according to the laws to which they have confented; an individual holding one acre, cannot encroach on him who has a thoufand, becaufe he is bound by the law which fecures property in this unequal manner. This is the municipal law of the ftate under which he lives. The member of a diftant fociety is not excluded by the laws from a right to the foil: He claims under the general law of nature, which gives a right, equally to all, to fo much of the foil as is neceffary for fubfiftance. Should a German from the clofely peopled country of the Rhine, come into Pennfylvania, more thinly peopled, he would be juftifiable in demanding a fettlement, though his perfonal force would not be fufficient

E   to

to effect it. It may be said that the cultivation or melioration of the earth, gives a property in it. No—if an individual has ingrossed more than is necessary to produce grain for him to live upon, his useless gardens, fields and pleasure walks, may be seized upon by the person who not finding convenient ground elsewhere, chooses to till them for his support.

It is a usual way of destroying an opinion, by pursuing it to its consequence. In the present case we may say, that if the visiting one acre of ground could give a right to it, the visiting a milion would give a right on the same principle; and thus a few surly ill natured men, might in the earlier ages, have excluded half the human race from a settlement, or should any have fixed themselves on territory, visited before they had set a foot upon it, they must be considered as invaders of the rights of others.

It is said that an individual, building a house or fabricating a machine has an exclusive right to it, and why not those who improve the earth? I would say, should a man build houses on a greater part of the soil than falls to his share, I would, in a state of nature, take away a proportion of the soil and the houses from him, but a machine or any work of art, does not lessen the means of subsistence to the human race, which an extensive occupation of the soil does.

Claims founded on the first discovery of soil are futile. When gold, jewels, manufactures, or any work of men's hands is lost, the finder is intitled to some reward, that is, he has some claim on the thing found, for a share of it.

When by industry or the exercise of genius, something unusual is invented in medicine or in other matters, the author doubtless has a claim to an exclusive profit by it, but who will say the soil is lost, or that any one can found a claim by discovering it. The earth with its woods and rivers still exists, and the only advantage I would allow to any individual for having cast his eye first on any particular part of it, is the privilege of making the first choice of situation. I would think the man a fool and unjust, who would exclude me from drinking the waters of the Mississippi river, because he had first seen it. He would be equally so who, would
exclude

exclude me from fettling in the country weft of the
Ohio becaufe in chafing a buffaloe, he had been firft o-
ver it.

The idea of an exclufive right to the foil in the natives had its origin in the policy of the firft difcoverers,
the kings of Europe. Should they deny the right of the
natives from their firft treading on the continent, they
would take away the right of difcovery in themfelves,
by failing on the coaft. As the veftige of the mokkifon
in one cafe gave a right, fo the cruize in the other was
the foundation of a claim.

Thofe who under thefe kings, derived grants, were
led to countenance the idea, for otherwife why fhould
kings grant or they hold extenfive tracts of country.

Men become enflaved to an opinion that has been
long entertained. Hence it is that many wife and good
men will talk of the right of favages to immenfe tracts
of oil.

What ufe do thefe ring ftreaked, fpotted and fpeckled
cattle make of the foil? Do they till it? Revelation
faid to man, " Thou fhalt till the ground." This a-
lone is human life. It is favourable to population, to
fcience, to the information of a human mind in the wor-
fhip of a God. Warburton has well faid, that before
you can make an Indian a chriftian you muft teach him
agriculture and reduce him to a civilized life. To live
by tilling is *more humano*, by hunting is *more beftarum*. I
would as foon admit a right in the buffaloe to grant
lands, as in Killbuck, the Big Cat, the Big Dog, or any
of the ragged wretches that are called chiefs and fa-
chems. What would you think of going to a big lick,
or place where the beafts collect to lick the faline and
nitrous earth and water, and addreffing yourfelf to a
great buffaloe to grant you land? It is true he could
not make the mark of the ftone or the mountain in his
deed ; but he could fet his cloven foot to the paper like
the great Ottoman, the father of the Turks, who when
he put his fignature to an inftrument, dipt his hand
and fpreading fingers in the ink and laid them on the
parchment. To fee how far the folly of mankind would
go, I had once a thought of fupplicating one of thefe
great elkes or buffaloes that run to the weftward, to
make me a grant of a hundred thoufand acres: I could
prove

prove he had brushed the weeds with his tail, and run fifty miles. I wonder if Congress or the different states would recognize the claim. I am so far from thinking the Indians have right to the soil, that not having made a better use of it for many hundred years, I conceive they have forfeited all pretence to claim, and ought to be driven from it.

With regard to forming treaties or making peace with this race, these are my ideas:—They have the shapes of men and may be of the human species, but certainly in their present state they approach nearer the character of Devils: take an Indian is there any faith in him? Can you bind him by favours? Can you trust his word or confide in his promise? When he makes war upon you, when he takes you prisoner and has you in his power will he spare you? In this he departs from the law of nature, by which, according to baron Montesquieu and every other man who thinks on the subject, it is unjustifiable to take away the life of him who submits; the conqueror in doing otherwise becomes a murderer, who ought to be put to death. On this principle are not the whole Indian nations murderers? Many of them may have not had an opportunity of putting prisoners to death, but the sentiment which they entertain leads them invariably to do this when they have it in their power or judge it expedient: these principles constitute them murderers, and they ought to be prevented from carrying them into execution, as we would prevent a common hommicide, who should be mad enough to conceive himself justifiable in killing men.

The tortures which they exercise on the bodies of their prisoners, justify extirmination. Gelo of Syracuse made war on the Carthaginians, because they offered up human victims, and made peace with them on condition they would cease from this unnatural and cruel superstition. If we could have any faith in the savages, I would suffer them to live, provided they would no longer make war amongst themselves, or against others, by lurking privately on the path ways of the wood, and putting unarmed and defenceless inhabitants to death, or attacking women and children in the frontier families, and on their ceasing in the mean to exercise torture.

'I do

I do not know but I ought to recal my word and say, that even reforming from these practices, they ought not to live: These nations are so degenerate from the life of man, so devoid of every sentiment of generosity, so prone to every vicious excess of passion, so faithless, and so incapible of all civilization, that it is dangerous to the good order of the world that they should exist in it. Why was it that a stream of fire was sent to burn up Sodom and Gomorrah, or some years before a deluge of water to wash the old world, but that the evil example of wicked men and horrid deeds might be struck from the knowledge and memory of the world? Why was it that the Canaanites were sentenced to extirpation, but because their rites and practices rendered them unfit to live. With what zeal did that good man Samuel hew Agag in pieces? With the same zeal ought every whig in America to hew the Big Pipe, or the Big Rattlesnake, or any of these, yclept by whatever name, wherever he can find them It may be said the Israelites had an order from the Lord to put to death the Canaanites. I think when we see men by their practice murderers, by every sentiment and principle of heart carried out to shed blood privately; it is a sufficient order to exterminate the whole brood. As the Seceder said of Satan, what will you make of them, my beloved, but ill, vile, evil devils?

There have been instances of several of these creatures that have been taken young from the woods, and put to public schools in America; I do not know one who has even by these means been rendered a useful member of society: They retain the temper of their race. I knew one of these, a certain John Montour, who had been educated at one of the northern seminaries, taught Greek and Latin, and in this war dignified by Congress with a commission of captain. No greater savage ever existed. He had murdered several of his own people, and being obliged to avoid the resentment of their relations, had fled from one place to another, and at last joined our arms at Fort Pitt. I saw this man with the bloody scalp of an Indian in his hand, which he had just taken off, having first tomhawked the creature, though submitting and praying for his life. The Indian had been for some time a prisoner with us, on

suspicion

suspicion of having acted against us, but having always professed himself a friend, and not being yet convicted of any murder, it was ruthful in his fellow savage to put him to death. I am well persuaded, that for a keg of whiskey you might induce any Indian to murder his wife, child, or best friend. I am informed, that the experiment was actually made by a trader. An Indian for a quart of whisky, in one of the western towns cut the throat of his own child.

This being the character of these men, shall we not wish to dispossess them of the goodly lands, springs and rivers to the westward, which they have so long made a scene of horror by their practices. At the termination of the present war, when they are no longer assisted by our enemies, it will be easy to drive them beyond the lakes: Instead of forming treaties, and sending any other talk to them, and prophaning ourselves by calling them brothers, I would simply let them know that they are no longer to show themselves below the heads of the great rivers that fall from the westward into the Ohio and Mississippi waters: After some period they may be reduced to more distant bounds, until driven to the cold snows of the north west, where darkness reigns six months in the year, if the continent extends so far, their practices shall be obscured, and the tribes gradually abolished.

H. BRACKENRIGE.